THIS NOTEBOOK BELONGS TO :

____